LEARNING WITH LETTS
For six- to seven-year-olds

The Project

Story by Irene Yates
Activities by David Bell, Geoff Leyland,
Mick Seller and Irene Yates

Illustrations by Pauline Little

People who live in Cherry Walk

For Lynn

Charley had big plans. He'd learned all about China at school.

'Hey Dad,' he yelled down the stairs. 'Can we go?'

Find China on a world map or a globe.
Talk about the different ways you could get there.

Try to remember a journey you have gone on recently on a bus or train or boat.
Were you going to see relatives or friends?
Or going shopping? Or going on holiday?

Write down three things about the journey for someone else to read.

'Not tonight son. It's the other side of the world,' said Dad.

'Dinner's ready!' called Mum from the kitchen. 'It's your favourite, Charley – get the chopsticks!'

What's your favourite meal? What different items of food do you need to make it?

What quantities of everything do you need if all the family are eating the meal? Supposing you invited two friends to the meal as well – how much more of the items would you need?

What kind of spoon is Dad using?
Is it a teaspoon or a tablespoon?
How many different sizes of spoon can you find at home?

Guess how many teaspoons of dry rice or sugar you need to fill a tablespoon. Now measure it out carefully. How good was your guess?

When your mum or dad is next cooking, have a look at what they measure with.
When do they use a teaspoon?
When do they use a tablespoon?

Charley stopped to think
'I know that, of course!'

'You could go and see Mrs Wilkins. She's the supermarket manager and she's a friend of mine,' Mum suggested.

What was Charley thinking about?

Do you dream about a journey you might make one day? Or about a magic journey? See if you can make up a story about it.
Record it on a tape recorder and then play it to someone in the family.

Mrs Wilkins was very keen to help with the project. Next day she collected Charley and Kerry and drove them to the supermarket.

What season do you think it is in the picture? What can you see that makes you think this?

What special clothes do you wear in that season? Do you eat different kinds of food? Are there any activities that you do then?

You could make a seasons chart. Write 'spring', 'summer', 'autumn' and 'winter' across the top of a piece of paper. In each column draw objects that belong to that season.

'What would you like?' smiled Betty at the delicatessen counter. 'Salami from Italy? Bacon from Denmark? Cheese from France?'

'Something from Germany please!' said Kerry. Betty wrapped a garlic sausage carefully in greaseproof paper.

'Mmmmm...'

How many things made of paper can you find in the picture? Which do you think is greaseproof paper?

Collect as many different kinds of paper as you can from around your home. Look at each of them closely. Crunch them up in your hand and listen to the sound they make.

Make a collage picture using the different types of paper you have collected.

Round the corner they found a boy stacking tins of sweetcorn.

'From America!' Charley hooted with glee. 'We'll take one!'

What might happen to the stack of tins if Kerry took hers from the bottom?
Is the stack taller or shorter than Charley?

See how tall a stack you can make on the floor. You could use dominoes, or tins, or other objects that are all the same size.
Try different ways of stacking.

Now see what happens if you use objects which are of different sizes, such as books or boxes.

At the dairy produce Kerry wrote lots of notes, while Charley read the labels.

Then he reached for some New Zealand butter.

Whoops!

What things made from milk can you see in the picture?
Do you know how any of them are made?

You can make your own butter at home.
Find a clean jar with a lid.
Half fill it with full-fat milk, and add a pinch of salt.
Now shake it for about 20 minutes.
You'll need someone to help you!

What has happened to the milk?

The children stared at the fish. The fish stared back.

'A tin of sardines from Portugal would be best for school,' said Mrs Wilkins.

'Get one from the shelf, then I'll take you home. I bet you're hungry after looking at all this food.'

Charley was *starving*.

Buy a whole fish, and look at it closely before it is cooked.
Look carefully at its head, tail, eyes and scales.
If you touch it wash your hands well afterwards.

Draw a picture of the fish. Put these words on your picture.

tail   scales   head   fins   mouth   eyes

That afternoon Kerry's mum took them to the market.

Charley was first to spot the potatoes.
'They're from Egypt!' he cried.
So they put some in a bag to be weighed.

The stall-holder sells all his vegetables by the pound (lb).
How much do the Egyptian potatoes cost?
Are they cheaper or more expensive than the English ones?
Why do you think this is?

Which is the cheapest vegetable on the stall?
Which is most expensive?

Kerry's mum wants to buy 1lb of carrots, 1lb of Brussels sprouts and 1lb of tomatoes. How much will that cost?
You can use a calculator to help you.

There were huge bunches of grapes from Spain, juicy oranges from Morocco, prickly pineapples from the Ivory Coast...

'... and bananas from Jamaica, where my grandad lives,' cried Charley.

'We'll have the biggest bunch you've got!'

Ask your mum or dad to cut an orange in half.
Look at it carefully.
Try making an orange print. Dip the cut surface
of the orange into some paint. Press it (not too hard!)
on to a piece of paper.
What does your print look like?

Try this with other fruits.
Which fruits are the best for printing?
Can you tell which fruit has been used to make each print?

While mum was choosing spices, the lady on the stall chatted to the children. She offered them some pumpkin seeds to taste.

'Mmmm . . .' said Kerry. 'Where are they from?'

'From a pumpkin,' the stall-holder grinned.

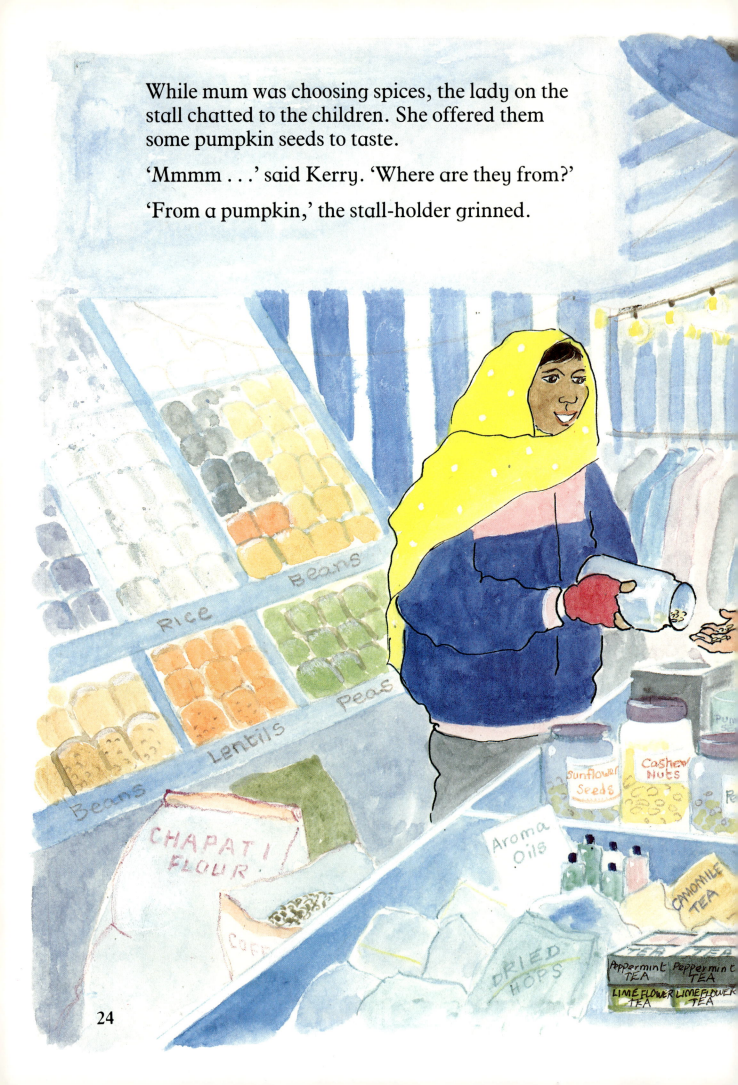

When your mum or dad is next cutting up fruit or vegetables, or you're eating them, look carefully inside.
Try looking at tomatoes, cucumbers, apples, grapes, plums.

Do they have a lot of seeds, a few – or just one?
Are the seeds large or small? What colour are they?

Collect some of the seeds and dry them.
Do they change at all?

You could try growing something from seed.
Ask your mum or dad to buy you some mung beans – these are the seeds from which beansprouts grow.

Mum wanted, 'Four ounces of lovely hot peppercorns all the way from India, please.'

'You mean 100 grams, don't you Mum,' said Kerry.

Do you think 100 grams is heavy or light?

Hold a potato in your hand. Does it weigh 100 grams?
Can you find one that does? Weigh it on your scales at home.

Now find a carrot and an onion.
How much do they each weigh? Guess first.

Guess how many tablespoons of rice weigh 100 grams.
Try guessing then weighing other dry things, such as salt, sugar and flour.

Do your guesses get better with practice?

Kerry invited Charley to tea.

'How about a cabbage from Britain for your collection?' said Mum. 'And it's free!'

What's happening in the picture? What time of day is it now? How do you think Kerry and Charley are feeling?

Read through the story again. See if you can remember all the things that Kerry and Charley have collected without looking at the book. Write them down as you remember them. Ask your mum or dad to have a go too. Can they remember more or less than you?

What was the best topic or project that you have done at school? Why did you like it? What project would you most like to do?

'We've got food from everywhere for our project, Dad!' said Kerry proudly.

'And here's some more,' laughed Dad, serving the tea.

'Just-a one-a spaghetti-a . . .'
'From Italy!' chorused the children.

And they all tucked in.

Have you heard of any of the countries mentioned in the story? See if you can find any of them on a globe or map of the world.

Have a look at the packets and tins of food in your kitchen cupboard and fridge. Look at the labels carefully to find out which countries the items came from. Are any of them the countries mentioned in the story? If they are different you could look for them on the globe or map too.

Activity notes

Pages 2–3 This activity encourages your child to remember and talk about personal experience. To add interest, they could draw a picture to go with their writing.

Pages 4–5 This activity is about the kind of estimating that adults do all the time. Helping to plan a meal at home will give your child valuable practice in everyday maths.

Pages 6–7 The guessing and checking in this activity are a practical way of developing estimating and basic measuring skills.

Pages 8–9 Most children love making up stories about magic or fantastic journeys. If you are going to record the story on tape, you'll probably want to help your child write it up first, so that they can concentrate on presenting the story for someone else to listen to.

Pages 10–11 In the first two years at school children often do topic work which is linked to a particular time of year. They may find it difficult to recall what happens in the other seasons. Recording information about the different seasons in the simple chart will help. You could make another chart together, this time concentrating on the foods that are associated with each season.

Pages 12–13 In this activity your child is encouraged to investigate paper. A good way to show that different kinds of paper have different properties and uses is to try to mop up some water with greaseproof paper, newspaper, an envelope and a piece of kitchen roll. Which works best?

Pages 14–15 Building stacks in different ways and with a variety of materials develops a sense of structure. Let your child experiment freely. Encourage them to talk about what they are doing. If your child has realised the importance of a broad base and stability, you could suggest experimenting further, this time building a house of cards.

Pages 16–17 It is easy to take food for granted. You could demonstrate the idea of a food chain by asking questions like these. 'Where does milk come from?' (Cows.) 'What do cows eat?' (Grass.) 'What makes grass grow?' (Soil, rain, sun.) Your child might like to do a series of drawings to illustrate this food chain.

Pages 18–19 Look closely at the fish together: encourage your child to think about the features of animals that live in water. What other creatures do they know that live in water? Help them with the labels. Recording what they see in carefully labelled diagrams is an important scientific skill.

Pages 20–21 At school children learn to use metric measures only, but for everyday maths it is important that children can do simple calculations based on both imperial and metric measures.

Pages 22–23 Making prints with different fruits is fun and helps children to get a feel for texture and shape, as well as observing and thinking about the qualities of different fruits. Which make the best prints: fruits with soft or firm flesh, fruits with lots of juice, etc?

Pages 24–25 This activity involves finding out about seeds: how they differ; how they change, etc. Growing new plants from seeds is the best way for your child to see the life cycle of a plant: seed – plant – flower – seed.
It will also help them to understand the right growing conditions for a plant.

Pages 26–27 Your child will automatically think that 100 grams must be a heavy weight because it is a high number. These practical weighing activities will help to develop more accurate estimating skills.

Pages 28–29 Remembering what the children in the story have collected is a good test of powers of recall. Your child will enjoy testing your memory as well!

Pages 30–31 Children can learn a lot about where different foods come from simply by looking at what you have in your store cupboards. Finding the country of origin on a world map will help develop their geography skills as well!

About the authors and advisers

Irene Yates is a writer and teacher in charge of language development at Lakey Lane School in Birmingham.

David Bell is Assistant Director of Education (Forward Planning) for Newcastle upon Tyne City Council, a former primary head and maths specialist.

Geoff Leyland is Deputy Head of Deer Park Primary School in Derbyshire and a former science and technology advisory teacher.

Mick Seller is Deputy Head of Asterdale Primary School in Derbyshire and a former science and technology advisory teacher.

Elizabeth Bassant is a language advisory teacher in Haringey, London. **Peter Ovens** is Principal Lecturer for Curriculum and Professional Development at Nottingham Polytechnic and a science specialist. **Peter Patilla** is a maths consultant, author and Senior Lecturer in Mathematics Education at Sheffield Polytechnic.

Margaret Williams is an advisory teacher for maths in Newton Abbott, Devon.